SELECTIONS FROM THE HOLY QURAN

FOR STUDENTS AND YOUTHS TO UNDERSTAND THE QURAN AND ITS TEACHINGS IN SIMPLE LANGUAGE

AFTAB ALAM KHAN

Dedicated

To

My wife, children, relatives and friends

who have always been a source of
motivation for me

Contents

Foreword

Selections From The Holy Quran

The Holy Quran is the last testament of Almighty God for the guidance of whole mankind. It was revealed upon Prophet Muhammad who was the last Messenger of God. It was revealed more than fourteen hundred years ago in the Arabic language which is a live language and is still spoken in Arabian countries.

This text is a compilation to address the needs of English-speaking students and youths of the present age who have no knowledge of the Arabic language or have time to read the translation of the Holy Quran, which contains more than six thousand verses. This booklet includes English translations of selected verses from the Holy Quran on various important topics covered in the Divine book. It is an attempt to present the teachings of the Quran on different subjects in a simple language. It also includes advice for achieving success in this world and in the Hereafter.

Preface

All praise is due to Allah, the Lord of the universe, the most Beneficent and Merciful, the Lord of the Day of Judgement. At the outset, I would like to thank the gracious God, who has once again provided me with an opportunity to present a book based on the Holy Quran. I have titled the book "Selection from the Holy Quran."

For the last few years, I have been sending the selected verses of the Quran with their translation in English and Hindi with the caption, "Today's Quote", every morning to my relatives, friends and acquaintances through WhatsApp messages. I am happy to learn that they like these messages, and some of them share these posts with others. My main objective has always been to convey the message and teachings of the Quran to as many people as possible using social media. For this, I have mainly used the English translation of Maulana Wahiduddin Khan Saheb, the renowned Islamic scholar, and the Hindi translation of Farooque Khan Saheb, which is available on the internet as a reference.

Such messages now crossed the 200 mark, so I thought of the need to organize all such messages in Hindi and English separately in book form, which may be of relevance for ordinary people, especially students and youths, to learn the fundamental teachings of the Quran. However, it is alway advisable to read the whole Quran directly to understand divine guidance.

During my study of Quran I found that Quran covers large number of topics to guide the humanity of all times, believers, nonbelievers, atheists, polytheists, Jews, Christians, educated, illiterates etc. Here I have tried to cover various topics in this book as per my understanding, like Monotheism, Prophethood, the Day of Judgement, Spirituality, Articles of faith, Obligatory Prayers, Zakat, Fasting, Hajj, Good deeds, Prohibited and permissible items, Social conduct, Morality, Family laws, Paradise, Hell, etc.

It's my humble effort to covey the message of the Quran to as many people as possible. I am very thankful to Almighty Lord for blessing me with this opportunity. I am also grateful to all my friends who have inspired me to undertake this work. My special thanks to my friend Dr Moin Qazi a renouned author, researcher, development professional and academician who went through the draft and gave useful suggestions.

Lastly, I pray to Allah to accept this small effort of mine, forgive me for any inadvertent mistake and make it a source of salvation for me. Also, I earnestly request the readers to please convey to me any errors found during reading that can be rectified in future editions.

Aftab Alam Khan
39, New Gandhi Lay out,
Jafar Nagar, Nagpur. INDIA. 440013
Contact No. Mob. 9421708641,
E. Mail: aftab.khan57@gmail.com

Acknowledgements

I am very thankful to the Almighty God for blessing me with this opportunity to compile this book for the youths and students. I am also grateful to all my friends who inspired me to undertake this work. My special thanks to my friend Dr Moin Qazi a renowned auther, researcher, development professsional and academician who went through the draft and offerred useful suggestions.

CHAPTER ONE

CONTENTS

Page No.

1. Signs of the existence of God are all around us
2. Allah controls every thing in the heavens and the earth
3. Do not make partners to Allah ....
4. God will surely test us during our life
5. On the Day of Judgment all deeds will be measured
6. Do not take two gods, and He is only one God
7. Do not worship anyone besides Allah
8. On the Judgment day no relationship would benefit
9. The disbelievers will be led towards Hell in groups
10. Believers will be greeted at the gate of Paradise
11. God created all humanity from one soul
12. Jinn and humanity should worship only Almighty God
13. God created man from moulded mud of clay
14. Allah is the First and the Last
15. Each one has to die and shall return to God
16. Description of the Day of Resurrection

1. God is with you where ever you are
2. Allah has excellent names, so glorify Him by any name
3. Qayamat and the Day of Judgement will indeed occur
4. On the day of Judgment, partner gods will reject their followers
5. Islam is the only religion acceptable to Allah
6. Who will be blessed with Paradise in the Hereafter?
7. God will not forgive those who make partners with Him
8. Five articles of Islamic faith
9. Allah has always appointed men as His Messengers
10. The Messengers speak in the language of the people
11. Jesus Christ was also a messenger of God
12. Do not differentiate among any of God's Messengers
13. Give full measure and weight
14. Pay back deposits to their rightful owners
15. Do not consume each other's wealth wrongfully
16. Avoid major sins which Allah forbids
17. Don't sit with the people who ridicule God's revelations
18. God knows everything hidden or open
19. Our life and death should be for Allah

1. Six qualities of good Muslims
2. God does not love the transgressors
3. Satan tempted Adam and his wife to disobey God
4. You will hear hurtful things from other people
5. Be tolerant and promote righteousness
6. Anyone who accepts guidance is for his own sake
7. Eight categories of persons eligible for zakat
8. Items that Allah prohibits

Chapter 8. 45

1. Do not worship the Sun and the Moon
2. No human can talk to Allah directly
3. Almighty God sent down the holy Quran
4. God gives life and death, and to Him we shall return
5. Think deeply over the verses of the Quran
6. Description of the Paradise
7. Do not believe any news unless you verify it
8. Try to make peace between believers
9. Allah is closer to us than our jugular vein
10. All misfortunes are as per the divine book
11. Angels of God also pray for the believers
12. Qualities of true believers
13. What is called supreme success?
14. God knows what is in every heart
15. Nothing happens by your will
16. God knows best who is rightly guided
17. Always be kind to your parents

Chapter 9. 51

1. Don't get divided into sects
2. Do not mix truth with falsehood
3. There is no coercion in religion
4. Always speak gently to your parents
5. Follow a middle path in your expenditure
6. Adultery is a great sin
7. There must be a group of reformers in the society
8. Pray to God. He will answer your prayer
9. God is truly bountiful to people
10. God says only, "Kun!" and it is done.
11. The Husband is the protector of his wife

12. Do not enter other's house with out permission
13. Qualities of good Muslims
14. Punishment for the disbelievers
15. God has made this earth our resting place
16. God is the most forgiving and ever-merciful
17. Do not despair of God's mercy
18. Dua of faithful believers before their Lord

1. Have faith in Allah and His Messenger
2. God has created everything for the service of humanity.
3. Help orphans and poor
4. All good things are made lawful for us
5. Those who disobey Allah and His Messenger shall enter the Hell
6. On Friday, rush for prayer when you hear Azan
7. Stand firmly for justice
8. God has no son and no partner to share His power
9. Creation of humans and their complete life cycle
10. Relationship with non-Muslims
11. Among Jews and Christians, there are some virtuous people
12. Evidence of the existence of God is available all around us
13. God has made the Sun and the moon to serve humanity
14. On Judgement day Prophet Christ will deny he is son of God

1. Do not compel anyone to accept Islam
2. Your wealth and children are only a test for you

Chapter 15. .... **86**

CHAPTER TWO

A BRIEF INTRODUCTION OF ISLAM

Islam is the second largest religion in the world after Christianity, with about 1.8 billion Muslims worldwide. There are 57 Islamic countries in the world, but Muslims are present in every country of the world, including the Arctic region. Islam has been the religion of Almighty God since the time of Prophet Adam and Mother Eve. The present version of Islam started in Maccah, Saudi Arabia, in the seventh century, with Prophet Muhammad, son of Abdullah bin Abdul Muttalib, as the Messenger of God. He is the last Messenger of Allah for the guidance of the humanity.

What is Islam?

The word "Islam" means "submission to the will of God," and the followers of Islam are called Muslims. Islam is a well-defined religion based on clear articles of faith, fundamental duties and elaborate guidelines for dos and don'ts that cover all essential facets of life. As per the Quran, only Islam is acceptable to Allah as a religion. (Innad deena indallahil Islam).

Fundamental Pillars of Islam:

There are three fundamental pillars of Islam, and without a firm belief in them, Islam is not complete.

1. **Monotheism**: It means belief in One Almighty God, the Creator and the Sustainer, the First and the Last, who is neither begotten nor has He fathered anyone. He is Supreme. Only He should be prayed for and worshipped without any partnership or association.

2.**Belief in the Qayamat and the Hereafter**: Present life given to human beings is temporary and limited and is a sort of test of their obedience to God. There is a time fixed by God to annihilate this world and all life on this planet. He has not disclosed its time of occurrence to anyone. This is called **Qayamat**. After some time, He will raise all humans again to evaluate their deeds. This is called the **Day of Judgment**. Virtuous people will be awarded with Paradise, and the sinful will be sent to Hell to face the punishment. Without belief in the Qayamat, the Day of Judgment and the Hereafter life, Islam is incomplete.

3.**Belief in the Messengers of God and Holy Books**: Muslims believe in all the Messengers of God, from Prophet Adam, who was the first Messenger of God, to Prophet Muhammad (peace be upon all of them), including Noah, Abraham, Ishaque, Yusuf, Jacob, Moses, Harun, Ayyub, Yunus, Daud, Solemon, Yahya, and Jesus Christ. The fundamental teachings of all the Messengers of God were the same: worship only Almighty God. Prophet Muhammad is the last Messenger of God for the guidance of humanity, and the Qur'an is the last book of God for the guidance of humankind.

- **Other articles of faith**:

In addition to the above-mentioned fundamental principles, there are some articles of faith in which Muslims firmly believe.

- **Belief in the angles**: As man is created from clay, Almighty God has created Angels from light, and they look after various jobs assigned by God.

- **Belief in the existence of the Paradise and the Hell.** On the Day of Judgment, the virtuous and sound will be blessed with the everlasting Paradise, and the evil and sinful will be awarded the eternal punishment of **Hell**.

- **Fundamental duties of Islam**: They include:

1. **Kalima. Shahadat**: to declare one's faith in God and belief in Muhammad. "There is no god to worship, but Allah and Prophet Muhammad is the Messenger of Allah".
2. **Salat or Namaz**: to pray five times a day (at dawn, noon, afternoon, sunset, and evening)
3. **Zakat**: to give in charity a portion of their wealth to the poor and needy.
4. **Sawm or Roza**: to fast during the month of Ramadan
5. **Hajj**: A pilgrimage to Makkah at least once during a person's lifetime if the person is capable of undertaking the journey and can afford expenditure.
6. Reading and understanding the Quran

7. **Noble deeds**: In the Quran, there are a large number of verses that deal with the subject of articles of faith and desirable noble deeds. It also contains the items that are prohibited in Islam. **PrincipleNoble deeds** include truthfulness, honesty, justice, equality, regular prayers, good moral conduct, show love and kindness to relatives, friends and others, obedience to parents, charity, mutual help, forbearance, thankfulness to God, etc.

The Holy Quran: Muslims believe that Almighty God revealed the Quran to Prophet Muhammad as the last divine book of guidance for humanity. Quran was first revealed in the month of Ramazan when he was in the cave Al-Hira near Maccah. At that time he was forty years old. It was revealed through the Angel Gabriel. Every Muslim has to memorize a small portion of the Quran as it is part of daily prayer. These verses are recited in Arabic only, which is the original language of the Quran.

Mosques: Mosques are the places where Muslims offer daily prayers and mass prayers like Fridays and Eid. As five times daily prayers are obligatory there are five times call for the Namaz or prayer which is called as Azan. For all namaz the timings are fixed for each mosque and they are sincerely followed. Namaz jamat is not delayed for any individual. Farz namaz is lead by the Imam of the mosque and in his absence any other respectable person can be the Imam. Although daily prayers can be performed at home, in the shops, offices or at any clean and peaceful place, mosque prayer is rated as better. The mosque premises is also used for teaching the Quran, religious preaching, Nikah functions and other social welfare programmes,

Holy Mosques: The Kaaba Mosque at Maccah, Saudi Arabia, is the greatest and the most sacred mosque for Muslims, where Muslims come from all over the world to perform the Hajj and Umrah pilgrimage. It was initially built by Prophet Abraham and his son, Prophet Ismail. Other holy places for Muslims include Prophet Muhammad's mosque in Medina, Masjid-e-Nabvi, and the Al-Aqsa mosque in Jerusalem.

Hadees: After the Quran, Hadees books are the primary source of guidance for Muslims, and they include the sayings and practices of Prophet Muhammad (pbuh) as narrated by his companions. There are six major Hadees books namely: Sahih Bukhari, Sahih Muslim, Sunan Abu Dawood, Sunan Al- Tirmidhi, Sunan Ibne Majah, and Muwatta Imam Malik.

Jihad: Jihad has been the most misunderstood word during the last few decades. Actually, it means to strive hard to achieve a noble goal, but this was erroneously linked with the holy war to malign Islam and Muslims. Islam is the religion of peace, and the life of Prophet Muhammad is the best example of this. The best Jihad is to fight the evil forces within oneself. And if a war is fought for the noble cause and justice, it is also a form of Jihad.

Equality: As all human beings are the children of Prophet Adam and Mother Eve, therefore all are relatives of each other, and they are equal. There is no discrimination among people on the basis of skin colour, race, place of birth, family, or tribe. This is best demonstrated in the daily prayers in mosques, where people, irrespective of race, region, or position, stand shoulder to shoulder under one Imam.

Islamic Calendar: The Islamic calendar, also called the Hijri calendar, is a lunar calendar used by Muslims for their religious celebrations. The calendar began in the year 622 A.D., celebrating the journey of Prophet Muhammad from Makkah to Medina.

Muslim Festivals: The two major Muslim festivals are:

1. **Eid ul-Fitr:** It is celebrated on the 1st of Shawwal, which is the tenth month of the Hijri calendar and at the end of Ramadan—the month of fasting. On this occasion, Muslims pay charity to the poor and needy in the form of Fitrah, offer mass prayer at Eidgah, put on new clothes and prepare delicious dishes, especially Sheer khurma, sewage and veg and non-veg items.

2. **Eid ul-Adha:** It is celebrated on the 10th day of Zilhajja, the twelfth month of the Hijri calendar. During this period, Hajj is performed in Maccah. Muslims in other places offer animal sacrifice; they keep a small portion of meat for their consumption and distribute the rest among relatives, friends and poor and needy as gift.

==============================

CHAPTER THREE

<u>Introduction of the Quran by its verses</u>

1.

First chapter of Quran, Sura Al-Fateha

In the name of Allah, the Most Gracious, the Most Merciful.

All praise is due to Allah, the Lord of the Universe; the Beneficent, the Merciful; the Lord of the Day of Judgement. You alone we worship, and to You alone we turn for help. Guide us to the straight path: the path of those whom You have blessed, not of those who have incurred Your wrath, nor of those who have gone astray. [Quran Chapter 1: 1-7]

2. The Quran is guidance for those who are mindful of God.

This is the Book; there is no doubt in it. It is a guide for those who are mindful of Allah, who believe in the unseen, and are steadfast in prayer, and spend out of what We have provided them with; those who believe in the revelation sent down to you and in what was sent before you, and firmly believe in the life to come. They are the people who are rightly following their Lord, and they shall be successful. [Quran Chapter 2: 2-5]

3. The Quran was revealed in the month of Ramazan.

The month of Ramadan is the month when the Quran was sent down as guidance for humanity with clear proofs of guidance, and it is the criterion by which to distinguish right from wrong. Therefore, whoever of you is present in that month, let him fast, but he who is ill or on a journey shall fast a similar number of days later on. God desires ease for you, not hardship. He desires you to fast the whole month, and you should glorify Him for His having guided you, and you should be grateful to Him. [Quran 2: 185]

4. The first five verses of the Quran as revealed

Read! In the name of your Lord, who created: 2. He created man from a clot [of blood]. 3. Read! Your Lord is the Most Bountiful One. 4. He taught by the pen. 5. He taught man what he did not know. [Quran Chapter 96]

5. Challenge of the Quran to humanity

If you are in doubt about the revelation We have sent down to Our servant, then produce a single chapter like it, and call upon your helpers besides God if you are truthful. But if you cannot do it, and you can never do it, then guard yourselves against the Fire whose fuel is men and stones, it is prepared for those who deny the truth [Quran Chapter 2: 23-24]

6. Severe punishment for those who reject the Quran.

God! There is no deity save Him, the Living, the Sustainer. He has sent down the Book to you with truth, which fulfils [the predictions] in the Scriptures that preceded it: He sent down the Torah and the Gospel in the past as guidance for humanity; He has sent down the Standard (The Quran) by which to discern the true from the false. Indeed, those who deny God's verses will suffer severe punishment. God is mighty and capable of retribution. [Quran Ch. 3 : 2 – 4]

7. Quran is a light for the guidance of the people.

(O Prophet) We have thus revealed a blessing (Quran) to you by Our command. And you knew neither the Scripture nor the faith, but We made it a light. We guide with it whoever We want from Our servants. You are indeed guiding me to the straight path. The path of God, to whom belongs all that is in the heavens and on the earth. Indeed, all matters are eventually decided by God. [Quran Chapter 42: 52-53]

8. The Quran is a reminder to the people.

43. So, hold firmly (the Quran) that has been revealed to you. You are indeed on the right path. 44. It is indeed a reminder to you and your people, and you will soon be questioned. [Quran Chapter 43]

9. The Quran is a book of enlightenment and guidance.

This [Quran] brings enlightenment and guidance to humanity and is a blessing for those who have firm faith. [Quran 45:20]

10.   There is no ambiguity in the Quran.

27. We have explained to men all kinds of examples in this Quran so that they may take lessons. 28. A Quran in Arabic, free from any ambiguity, so that people may be mindful of God. [Quran Chapter 39]

11.   Quran is the divine book for the humanity

God has sent down the best message: a similar scripture that is oft-repeated, which causes trembling in those who fear their Lord. And their skins and their hearts soften at the mention of God: such is God's guidance. He guides with this (Quran) whomsoever He wills, but no one can guide those whom God leaves to stray. [Quran 39:23]

===================================

CHAPTER FOUR

In the name of Allah, the Most Gracious and Merciful.

1. Signs of the existence of God are all around us.

Another of His signs is that He created the heavens and earth and the diversity of your languages and colours. There indeed are signs in this for those who have knowledge. Among His signs is your sleep, at night or in the daytime, and your seeking His bounty. There indeed are signs in this for people who hear. Among His signs is this: He shows you the lightning, giving rise to [both] fear and hope, and rains water from the sky, giving life thereby to the earth after it had been lifeless. Indeed, there are signs for people who use their reason! Another of His signs is this: the heavens and the earth stand firm by His command, and afterwards, when He calls you (on the day of resurrection), you will come forth from the world. [Quran Chapter 30: 22-25]

2. Allah controls everything in the heavens and the earth.

It was God who created the heavens and the earth, and whatsoever is in between them in six days, and then He established Himself on the throne. You have no patron or any intercessor besides Him (to help you). So, will you not pay heed? He directs all affairs from heaven to earth. Then all will again ascend to Him on a Day whose length is a thousand years by the way you count. Such is (your Lord) the Knower of the unseen and the visible, the Powerful, the Merciful.

[Quran Chapter 32: 4-6]

3. Do not make partners to Allah.

O' People, worship your Lord, who created you and those before you, so that you may become righteous, He made the earth a bed, and the sky a canopy; and it is He who sends down rain from above for the growth of every kind of food items for your sustenance. So, do not knowingly make partners with Allah.

[Quran Chapter 2: 21-22]

4. God will surely test us during our life.

We shall certainly test you with fear and hunger and loss of property, lives and crops. Give good news to those who endure with fortitude. Those who say, when afflicted with a calamity, "We belong to God and to Him we shall return"

[Quran Chapter 2: 155-156]

5. On the Day of Judgment, all deeds will be measured

An accurate scale will be set on that Day. Then, those whose scales are heavy shall be successful, and those whose good deeds are light [in the balance] will be the losers because they wrongfully rejected Our commandments.

[Quran Chapter 7: 8-9]

6. Do not take two gods. He is only one God.

God says, "Do not take two gods. He is only One God. So fear Me alone." To Him belongs whatsoever is in the heavens and on the earth, and obedience is due to Him alone. Will you then fear anyone other than God?
[Quran Chapter 16: 51-52]

7. Do not worship anyone besides Allah.

God has given you wives from among yourselves, and given you children and grandchildren from your wives, and provided wholesome things for you. Will they then believe in falsehood and deny God's favours? They worship, instead of God, things that have no control over their provision from the heavens or the earth in any way, nor do they have any power [to do so]. [Quran Chapter 16: 72-73]

8. On Judgment Day, no relationship would benefit

When the trumpet is blown, on that day, there will be no ties or relationships between them; neither will they ask about one another. Those whose scales weigh heavy with suitable work will be successful. But those whose scales weigh light will have ruined their souls; in Hell will they reside. [Quran 23: 101-103]

9. The disbelievers will be led towards Hell in groups

71. Those who rejected the truth will be led to Hell in groups. When they reach it, its gates will be opened, and its keepers will say to them, "Have messengers not come to you from among yourselves, who conveyed to you the revelations of your Lord and warned you about meeting [Him] on this Day?" They will answer, "Yes, they did

come." But the decree of punishment has proved true against the deniers of the truth. 72. They will be told, "Enter the gates of Hell, to stay therein forever." What an evil dwelling place for the haughty. [Quran Chapter 39]

10. Believers will be greeted at the gate of Paradise by 'Salam.'

But those who fear their Lord will be led in groups towards Paradise. When they reach it, its gate will be opened, and its keepers will say to them, "Peace be upon you. You have done well; enter Paradise and dwell in it forever." And they will say, "Praise be to God who has fulfilled His promise to us and made us the inheritors of this land, letting us settle in the Garden wherever we want." How excellent is the reward of those who did good deeds? [Quran Chapter 39: 73-74]

11. God has created all humanity from one soul

O' Mankind! Fear your Lord, who created you from a single soul. He created its mate from it, and from the two of them, countless men and women spread [throughout the earth]. Fear God, in whose name you appeal to one another, and be mindful of your obligations with respect to ties of kinship. God is always watching over you. [Quran 4:1]

12. God created Jinn and humanity so that they should worship Him

And keep on reminding them, for indeed, the reminder benefits the believers. 56. And I created the jinn and humanity so that they should worship Me. [Quran Chapter

51: 55]

13. God created man from moulded mud of clay.

We created man out of dry clay, from moulded mud, and the jinn We had created before from flaming fire. [Quran Chapter 15: 26-27)]

14. Allah is the First and the Last

Everything in the heavens and earth glorifies God, And He is the Mighty, the Wise One. He has sovereign control over the heavens and the earth. He gives life and brings death. He has power over all things. 3. He is the First and the Last, the Apparent and the Hidden. He knows all things. [Quran Chapter 57:1-2]

15. Each one has to die and shall return to God.

Every soul shall taste death, and then to Us you shall return. Those who believe and do good works, We shall lodge them in the mansions of Paradise, beside which rivers flow, and they shall be there forever. How excellent is the reward for those who do good deeds and who are steadfast and put their trust in their Lord? [Quran 29: 57-59]

16. Description of the Day of Resurrection

The Trumpet shall be blown, and whoever is in heaven and whoever is on earth will fall dead, except whom Allah wills. Then the trumpet will be blown again, and they shall rise and gaze around them. The earth will shine with the light of its Lord, and the record (of deeds) will be placed;

the prophets and witnesses will be brought in; and judgement will be passed on them with fairness. And none shall be wronged. Every soul will be repaid in full for what it has done. He is fully aware of all that they did. [Quran Chapter 39: 68-70]

==============================

CHAPTER FIVE

In the name of Allah, the most Beneficent and Merciful

1. God is with you wherever you are

It was He who created the heavens and earth in six Days [periods] and then ascended the throne. He knows what enters the earth and what comes out of it; what descends from the sky and what ascends to it. He is with you wherever you are; He sees all that you do. He has sovereignty over the heavens and the earth. God manages all affairs. [Quran Chapter 57: 4-5]

2. Allah has excellent names, so glorify Him by any name.

He is God; there is no deity save Him, the Sovereign, the Most Pure, the Source of Peace, the Granter of Security, the Protector, the Mighty, the Subduer, the Supreme. Glory be to God, who is far above what they associate with Him. He is God, the Creator, the Originator, the Giver of form. For Him, there are excellent names. Everything in the heavens and earth glorify Him. He is the Mighty, the Wise One. [Quran Chapter 59 : 23-24]

3. Qayamat and the Day of Judgement will indeed occur

Indeed, they are the losers who deny the meeting with God. And when the Hour (Qayamat) would come to them suddenly, they would cry, "Alas for us, that we neglected it!" They shall bear their burden on their backs. Evil is the burden they will bear. The life of this world is but insignificant and a pastime. Indeed, the Home of the Hereafter is best for those who fear God. So, will you not use your mind? [Quran Chapter 6: 31-32]

4. On the day of Judgment, partner gods will reject their followers.

On the Day when We gather them all together, We shall say to those who ascribed partners to God, "Keep to your places, you and your partners!" Then We shall separate them from one another, and their partner-gods will say, "It was not us that you worshipped. God suffices as a witness between us and you. We were entirely unaware that you worshipped us." [Quran Chapter 10: 28-29]

5. Islam is the only religion acceptable to Allah.

The only true religion acceptable to Allah is Islam. And those who were given the Book (Jews and Christians) disagreed only out of rivalry and after knowledge had come to them. He who denies God's verses should know that God is swift in His reckoning and evaluation. [Quran Ch. 3: 19]

6. Who will be blessed with Paradise in the Hereafter?

Those who spend in charity, both in prosperity and adversity, restrain their anger and are forgiving towards their fellow men, and God loves those who do good deeds. And who, when they have committed an indecency or have wronged their souls, remember God and pray that their sins be forgiven. And who can forgive sins but Allah. And they do not knowingly persist in their misdeeds. Their recompense is forgiveness from their Lord and Gardens with rivers flowing through them, where they will abide forever. How excellent will the reward be for those who do good deeds? [Quran 3: 134- 136]

7. God will not forgive those who make partners with Him

Indeed, God will not forgive the ascribing of partners to Him. He forgives whoever He will for anything other than that. And whoever ascribes partners to God has strayed far indeed. [Quran 4:116]

8. Five articles of Islamic faith

O' Believers believe in God and His Messenger and in the Scripture He sent down to His Messenger, as well as what He sent down before. He who denies God, His angels, His Scriptures, His messengers and the Last Day has undoubtedly gone far astray. [Quran 4:136]

9. Allah has always appointed men as His Messengers.

Before you, the messengers We sent were but men to whom We sent revelation. Ask the People of the Book if you do not know. [We sent them] with clear signs and scriptures. We have sent down the Reminder (Quran) to you to enable you to make clear to humanity what has been sent down to them so that they may reflect upon it. [Quran Chapter 16: 43-44]

10. The messengers of God speak in the language of the people.

Each messenger We have sent has spoken in the language of his people so that he might make the message clear to them. But God lets go astray whom He wants and guides whom He pleases. He is the Almighty, the All-Wise. We sent Moses with Our signs, saying, "Lead your people out of the darkness into the light and remind them of divine anecdotes. In that, there are signs for every patient and grateful person." [Quran Chapter 14: 4-5]

11. Jesus Christ was also a messenger of God.

People of the Book! Do not go to extremes in your religion. Say nothing but the truth about God. Christ Jesus, son of Mary, was only a messenger of God, and His word was conveyed to Mary as a spirit from Him. So believe in God and His messengers and do not say: "There are three [gods]." Desist; it will be better for you. Indeed, God is the one and only God. His Holiness is far above having a son. To Him belongs whatever is in the heavens and whatever is on the earth. And God is sufficient as a guardian. [Quran 4:171]

12. Do not differentiate among any of God's Messengers

The Messenger believes in what has been sent down to him from his Lord, and [so do] believers. They all believe in God and His angels, His scriptures, and His messengers. They say, "We do not differentiate between any of His messengers. We hear and obey. Grant us Your forgiveness, Lord, to You we shall all return!" [Quran 2:285]

13. Give full measure and do justice

Stay well away from an orphan's property, except with the best intentions, before he comes of age. Give full measure and weight, according to justice. We never charge a soul with more than it can bear, and when you speak, observe justice, even though it concerns a close relative, and fulfil the covenants of God. That is what He has enjoined upon you so that you may take heed. [Quran 6:152]

14. Payback deposits to their rightful owners

God commands you to pay back deposits to their rightful owners, and when you judge between people, you should judge with fairness. God's instructions to you are excellent. God hears and sees all things. [Quran 4:58]

15. Do not consume each other's wealth wrongfully.

O' Believers do not wrongfully consume each other's wealth but trade with it by mutual consent. Do not kill yourself, for God is most merciful to you. 30. If anyone does these things through transgression and injustice, We shall cast him into the Fire, and that is easy for God. [Quran Chapter 4: 29-30]

16. Avoid the great sins that Allah forbids.

If you shun the great sins you have been forbidden, We shall remove your minor misdeeds and admit you to a place of honour. [Quran 4:31]

17. Don't sit with the people who ridicule Quran

He has instructed you in the Book that when you hear people deny or ridicule God's revelations, you must not sit with them unless they engage in other talk, or else you shall become like them. God will gather all the hypocrites and those who deny the truth together in Hell. [Quran 4:140]

18. God knows everything hidden or open

He holds the keys to the unseen; none knows them but He. He knows all that land and sea contain. No leaf falls without His knowledge, nor is there a single grain in the darkness of the earth, or anything, wet or dry, but is recorded in a clear Record. [Quran 6:59]

19. Our life and death should be for Allah.

Say, "My prayer and my sacrifice and my life and my death are all for God, the Lord of the worlds; He has no partner. So am I commanded, and I am the first of those who submit to Him." [Quran 6: 162-163]

=========================

CHAPTER SIX

In the name of Allah, the most Beneficent and Merciful

1. Six qualities of good Muslims

The believers, both men and women, are friends to each other; they enjoin what is good and forbid evil. They attend to their prayers, pay the alms, and obey God and His Messenger. God will have mercy upon them. Indeed, God is almighty and wise. [Quran Chapter 9: 71]

2. God does not love the transgressors.

Call on your Lord with humility and in secret. He does not love the transgressors: And do not spread corruption on the earth after it has been set in order. Pray to Him with fear and hope. God's mercy is close to those who do good deeds. [Quran Chapter 7: 55- 56]

3. Satan tempted Adam and his wife to disobey God.

To Adam, He (Allah) said, "You and your wife dwell in the Garden and eat and drink there from wherever you wish, but do not approach this tree, lest you become wrongdoers." But Satan tempted them so that he might reveal to them their nakedness, which had been hidden from them. He said, "Your Lord has forbidden you to approach this tree lest you should become angels or become of the immortals," and he swore to them, "Surely, I am your well-wisher." [Quran Chapter 7:19-21]

4. You will hear hurtful things from other people

You will indeed be tried and tested in your possessions and your persons, and you shall surely hear many hurtful things from those who were given the Book before you and from those who set up partners with God. Still, if you endure with fortitude and restrain yourselves, that indeed is a matter of strong determination. [Quran Chapter 3: 186]

5. Be tolerant and promote righteousness

Be tolerant, enjoin what is right, and avoid the ignorant. If an evil impulse from Satan provokes you, seekrefuge with God; He is all-hearing and all-knowing. [Quran Chapter 7: 199- 200]

6. Anyone who accepts guidance is for his own sake.

[O Prophet], Say, "O' Mankind, Truth has come to you from your Lord! Anyone who accepts guidance is guided only for his own sake, and he who goes astray does so at his peril. I am not appointed as your protector." Follow what is revealed to you, [O Prophet], and be steadfast until God gives His judgement. He is the Best of Judges. [Quran Chapter 10: 108-109]

7. Eight categories of persons eligible for zakat

Alms are only for the poor and the destitute, for those who collect zakat, and for conciliating people's hearts, and for freeing enslaved people, and for those in debt, and spending for God's cause, and travellers in need. It is a legal obligation enjoined by God. God is all-knowing and wise. [Quran Chapter 9: 60]

8. Items that Allah prohibits

He has forbidden you only carrion, blood, and the flesh of swine; also, any item that is consecrated to other than God. But for one who is driven by necessity, neither craving nor transgressing, it is no sin. For God is forgiving and merciful. [Quran Chapter 2: 173]

9. God created heavens and the earth in six days

Indeed, your Lord is God who created the heavens and the earth in six days [periods], then He ascended the Throne, and He plans and manages everything. No one may intercede with Him save with His permission. Such is God, your Lord, so worship Him alone. So will you not take heed? [Quran 10: 3]

10. There are signs in the heavens and earth to know God

It is He who made the sun radiate a brilliant light, and the moon shed its lustre and ordained for it stages so that you may learn to count out the years and [to make other such] reckoning of time. God has not created all these without a purpose. He clearly explains His revelations to men of understanding. Indeed, in the alternation of night and day and in all that God has created in the heavens and the earth, there are signs of a God-fearing people. [Quran Chapter 10: 5-6]

11. Only Allah decides what is lawful or unlawful

Say, "Have you considered the provision God has provided to you, and you have made some of it unlawful and some lawful?" Ask them, "Has God given you permission [to do this], or are you fabricating falsehoods about God?" What will they think, who tell falsehoods about God, on the Day of Resurrection? Indeed, God is bountiful to men, yet most of them are not grateful. [Quran 10: 59-60]

12. God makes rulers to whomsoever He pleases

Say, "Lord, sovereign of all sovereignty. You bestow sovereignty upon whom You will and take it away from whom You please; You exalt whoever You will and abase whoever You will. All that is good lies in Your hands. Indeed, You have the power over anything. [Quran 3:26]

13. Never support an evil deed

Whoever supports a good cause shall have a share in its blessing, and whoever supports an evil cause shall be answerable for his part in it: for, indeed, God is watchful of everything. [Quran 4:85]

14. Ward off evil with good

Those who are steadfast in seeking the favour of their Lord and pray regularly and spend secretly and openly out of what We have provided them with, and ward off evil with good. Theirs shall be the final abode. They shall enter the eternal Gardens, along with the righteous from among their fathers, wives and descendants. From every gate, the angels will come to (greet) them. Peace be upon you for what you patiently endured. And excellent is the final home. [Quran Chapter 13: 22-23]

15. If you are grateful to God, He will give you more.

Remember also the time when your Lord declared, 'If you are grateful, I will surely bestow more favours on you; but if you are ungrateful, then know that My punishment is severe indeed.'" [Quran 14:7]

16. Pray to Allah for yourself and your children

My Lord, make me regular in the prayer, and so may my offspring. My Lord, You accept my prayer. [Quran 14:40]

17. God prescribed fasting for believers to purify them

O' Believers, fasting has been prescribed for you, just as it was prescribed for those before you, so that you may guard yourselves against evil. Fast for a specified number of days, but if anyone among you is ill or on a journey, let him fast for the same number of days later. For those who have the capacity, there is a way to compensate by feeding a needy person. But if one feeds more than one of his own accord, he shall be well rewarded, but fasting is better for you if you know. [Quran Chapter 2: 183-184]

18. Six Commands of God for Muslims

God commands justice and kindness and gives them [due to] near relatives, and He forbids all shameful deeds, injustice and transgression. He admonishes you so that you may take heed! [Quran 16:90]

19. Do not break your promise and pledge.

Fulfil the covenant of God when you have made one, and do not break your pledges after their confirmation. Indeed, you have made God your surety, for God knows all that you do. [Quran 16:91]

20. If you are forced to sin, God may forgive you

As for one who denies God after he has believed, with the exception of one who is forced to do it, while his heart rests securely in faith, but one who opens his heart to a denial of truth shall incur the wrath of God; such as these will have a terrible punishment. [Quran 16:106]

========================

CHAPTER SEVEN

In the name of Allah the most Beneficent and Merciful

1. You may invoke Allah by any suitable name.

Say, "Whether you invoke God or the Merciful One, His are the finest names." Pray neither in a voice that is too loud nor in silence, but follow a middle path between them. [Quran Chapter 17: 110]

2. Allah is the Lord of the universe, so invoke Him only.

He makes the night pass into the day, and He makes the day pass into the night. He has designed the sun and the moon, each running for an appointed term. Such is God, your Lord: He is the kingdom. Those whom you invoke besides Him do not own so much as the skin of a date stone. If you invoke them, they do not hear your supplication, and even if they could hear, they would not respond to you. And on the Day of Resurrection, they will disown you, having associated them with God. No one can tell you [the Truth] like the One who is all-knowing. [Quran Chapter 35:13-14]

3. Allah has no son and no partner.

And say, "All praise is due to God who has never begotten a son and who has no partner in His kingdom; nor does anyone aid Him because of any weakness of His. So proclaim His greatness." [Quran 17: 111]

4. Iman and good deeds both are necessary for success

And he who does good works and is a believer, he shall fear no harm nor any injustice." We have thus sent down the Quran in Arabic and given all kinds of warnings so that they may fear God or take heed. [Quran Chapter 20: 112-113]

5. On Judgement day, Allah will set up scales of justice

We shall set up scales of justice on the Day of Judgment so that no soul can be in the least wronged. Actions as small as a grain of mustard seed shall be weighed. And We are sufficient as a reckoner. [Quran 21:47]

6. God gives wealth to whom He pleases

If you ask them who it is that has created the heavens and the earth and subjugated the sun and the moon, they will say, "God."Then why do they turn away (from the right path)? God gives provisions abundantly to whom He wants and limits to whom He pleases. Indeed, God has full knowledge of all the things. [Quran Chapter 29:61-62]

7. God created everything in this world with a purpose

Do they not contemplate within themselves? God has created the heavens and the earth and all that is between them for a purpose and a specified term. Yet many deny they will ever meet with their Lord. [Quran 30:8]

8. Allah causes the rains to fall wherever He pleases

It is God who sends out the winds so that they raise the clouds. Then He spreads them in the sky as He wills and places them layer upon layer, and you see the rain coming forth from their midst. Then He causes it to fall on whichever of His servants He pleases. Then they rejoice; Although before that, before it was sent down upon them, they were in despair. Look, therefore, at the signs of God's mercy, how He resurrects the earth after its death. Indeed, the same God will resurrect the dead, for He has power over all things. [Quran Chapter 30: 48-50]

9. Our Belief and good deeds can bring us close to God

It is not your wealth or your children that will confer on your nearness to Us. It is those who believe and act righteously who will be doubly rewarded for their good deeds and will dwell in peace in the high pavilions [of paradise]. [Quran 34:37]

10. The sun and moon revolve in their orbits designed by God

The sun too, follows its determined course laid down for it by the Almighty, the All-Knowing. We have ordained phases for the moon until finally, it becomes like an old date-stalk. The sun cannot overtake the moon, nor can the night outpace the day: each one revolves in [its own] orbit. [Quran Chapter 36: 38-40]

11. The first house built for the Pilgrimage is at Makkah

The first House built for humanity (for Hajj) is the one at Bakkah [Makkah]. It is a blessed place, a source of guidance for the whole world. There are clear signs in it; it is the place where Abraham stood. Anyone who enters it will be secure. Pilgrimage to the House is a duty to God for anyone who is able to undertake it. Anyone who disbelieves should remember that God is not dependent on anyone in the world. [Quran Chapter 3: 96- 97]

12. Precautions during the Hajj pilgrimage

The pilgrimage is in the appointed months. So whoever intends to perform it during them must abstain from indecent speech, from all wicked conduct, and from quarrelling while on the pilgrimage. Whatever good you may do, God is aware of it. Make provisions for yourselves, but indeed, the best of all is a provision that is God-conscious. Always be mindful of Me, you who are endowed with understanding. [Quran Chapter 2: 197]

13. The complete life cycle of man

O' people! If you are in doubt about the Resurrection, remember that We first created you from clay, then from a sperm-drop, then from clotted blood, then a lump of flesh, both shaped and unshaped, so that We might manifest to you [Our power]. And We keep you in the womb for an appointed time, then We bring you forth as infants, and then We cause you to grow and reach full growth. Then, some of you pass away early in life, while some of you reach extreme old age, in which they know nothing of what they once knew. And you see the earth, dead and barren, but no sooner do We send down rain upon it than it begins to stir and swell and produce every kind of luxuriant vegetation. That is because God is the truth. It is He who gives life to the dead, and He has the power over everything. [Quran 22: 5-6]

14. Call people towards Allah, but don't argue with them

We have appointed for every community ways of worship to observe. Let them not dispute this matter with you. Call them to the path of your Lord, for indeed, you are rightly guided. If they should dispute with you, then say, "God is well aware of what you do." [Quran Chapter 22: 67-68]

15. Establish prayers and do good deeds to achieve success

O believers, bow and prostrate and worship your Lord and do good deeds - so that you may succeed. And strive for Allah with the striving due to Him. He has chosen you and has not placed any difficulty upon you in the religion. [It is] the religion of your father, Abraham. Allah named you "Muslims" before [in the former scriptures] and in this [revelation] so that the Messenger may be a witness over you and you may be witnesses over the people. So, establish prayer, give zakat, and hold firmly to Allah. He is your protector. He is an excellent protector and an excellent helper. [Quran Chapter 22: 77-78]

16. Good qualities of the believers

They (believers) tremble with fear of their Lord and believe in His messages. And they do not ascribe partners to Him. And they give to others what has been bestowed upon them, and their hearts trembling at the thought that they will surely return to their Lord. It is they who vie with one another in doing good works and want to be the foremost in doing so.

[Quran 23: 57-60]

========================

CHAPTER EIGHT

In the name of Allah, the most Beneficent and Merciful

1. Do not worship the Sun and the Moon.

Among His signs are the night and the day and the sun and the moon. Do not prostrate yourselves before the sun and the moon, but prostrate yourselves before God who created them all if it is truly Him that you worship. If they grow arrogant, [remember that] those who are with your Lord glorify Him night and day and never grow tired. [Quran Chapter 41: 37-38]

2. No human can talk to Allah directly.

It is not granted to any human being that God should speak to him other than by revelation or from behind a veil or by sending him a messenger so that the messenger may reveal, by His command, whatsoever He will. Indeed, He is exalted and wise. [Quran 42:51]

3. **Almighty God sent down the holy Quran.**

This Scripture is sent down from God, the Mighty and Wise One. Indeed, there are signs in the heavens and the earth for those who believe: And in your creation and all the creatures He has spread about, there are signs for people of sure faith; And in the succession of night and day, and in the means of subsistence which God sends down from the skies, giving life thereby to the earth after it had been lifeless, and in the circulation of the winds: [in all this] there are signs for people who use their reason. [Quran Chapter 45: 2-5]

4. God gives life and death, and to Him we shall return.

They say, "There is nothing but our life in this world: we die, and we live here. Nothing but time destroys us." They do not know of this; they only follow conjecture. And whenever Our clear revelations are recited to them, their only argument is to say, "Bring back to us our forefathers, if what you say is true." Say, "God gives you life, then causes you to die, and then He will gather you together on the Day of Resurrection, about which there is no doubt. But most people do not know it." [Quran Chapter 45:24-26]

5. Think deeply over the verses of the Quran.

Will they not ponder over this Quran? Or are there locks upon their hearts? Surely, those who turn their backs [on this message] after guidance has been shown to them, [do it because] Satan has embellished their fancies, and for them, there is a respite (for some time). [Quran Chapter 47:24-25]

6. Description of the Paradise

Here is a description of the Paradise promised to the righteous: therein are rivers of water which is forever pure; and rivers of milk of which the taste never changes; and rivers of wine, a delight to those who drink it, and rivers of pure honey. And in it, they will have all kinds of fruit and will receive forgiveness from their Lord. Can those who enjoy such bliss be like those who abide in the Fire and who are given boiling water to drink so that it tears their bowels? [Quran Chapter 47: 15]

7.   Do not believe any news unless you verify it

O' Believers, if an incredible person brings you news, then ascertain the correctness of the information thoroughly, lest you unwittingly harm others, and then regret what you have done. [Quran 49:6]

8.   Try to make peace between believers

Indeed, all believers are brothers. So make peace between your brothers, and fear God so that mercy may be shown to you. [Quran 49:10]

9.   Allah is closer to us than our jugular vein.

Indeed, We created man, and We know the promptings of his soul and are closer to him than his jugular vein. And the two recording angels are recording, sitting on the right and the left. Each word he utters is noted down by a vigilant guardian (angel). [Quran Ch. 50: 16-18]

10.   All misfortunes are as per the divine book.

No misfortune can affect the earth or your selves without its first having been recorded in a book before We bring it into being. That is easy for God to do. So do not grieve for what you have lost, nor be exultant over what you have gained. God loves neither the proud nor the boastful. [Quran Chapter 57: 22-23]

11. Angels of God also pray for the believers

Those who bear the Arsh (throne), and those who are around it glorify their Lord with His praise and believe in Him. They ask forgiveness for those who believe, saying, "Our Lord, You embrace all things in mercy and knowledge. Forgive those who turn to You and follow Your path. Save them from the punishment of Hell. And admit them, Lord, to the Eternal Garden You have promised to them, together with their righteous ancestors, spouses, and offspring: You alone are the Almighty, the All-Wise. [Quran Chapter 40: 7-8]

12. Qualities of true believers

Virtue does not consist in whether you face towards the East or the West; virtue means believing in God, the Last Day, the angels, the Book and the prophets; the virtuous are those who, despite their love for it, give away their wealth to their relatives and orphans and the very poor, and to travellers and those who ask [for charity], and to set enslaved people free. And who attend to their prayers and pay the alms, and who keep their pledges when they make them, and show patience in hardship and adversity, and in times of distress. Such are the true believers, and such are the God-fearing. [Quran 2:177]

13. What is called supreme success?

When He shall gather you all on the Day of Gathering that will be the Day of loss and gain; and whoever believed in God and did good deeds, his sins shall be forgiven, and he will be admitted to Gardens through which rivers flow, where they shall dwell forever. That is the supreme success. [Quran 64:9]

14. God knows what is in every heart.

Whether you speak in secret or aloud, He knows what is in every heart. How could He who created not know His creation? He alone is the Most Subtle in His wisdom and the All Aware. [Quran Ch. 67: 13-14]

15. Nothing happens by your will

Indeed, this (Quran) is a reminder. Let whoever wishes to take the right path to his Lord. Nothing happens by your will unless God wills. God is indeed all-knowing and wise. 31. He admits that whoever He wills is in His grace, and He has prepared a painful punishment for the evil doers. [Quran Chapter 76:29-31]

16. God knows best who is rightly guided

He who has entrusted you with the responsibility of the Quran will surely lead you to a successful end. Say, "My Lord knows best who is rightly guided and who is in gross error." You never expected that this Book would be revealed to you. Yet, by the grace of your Lord, you have received it. So do not support those who reject the truth. [Quran Chapter 28: 85-85]

17. Always be kind to your parents

We have encouraged the man to show kindness to his parents. But if they bid you to associate with Me something about which you have no knowledge, do not obey them. To Me you shall all return, and I shall tell you about all that you have done. [Quran 29:8]

==========================

CHAPTER NINE

In the name of Allah, the most Beneficent and Merciful

1. **Don't get divided into sects**

Hold fast to the cord of God (Quran), and let nothing divide you. Remember the blessings He has bestowed upon you. You were enemies, and then He united your hearts and by His grace, you became brothers; you were on the brink of an abyss of Fire, and He rescued you from it. Thus, God makes His signs clear to you so that you may find guidance. [Quran 3:103]

2. Do not mix truth with falsehood

Do not mix truth with falsehood or hide the truth when you know it. Attend to your prayers, give the zakat [prescribed alms] and bow down with those who bow down. [Quran Chapter 2:42-43]

3. **There is no coercion in religion.**

There shall be no compulsion in religion: the trustworthy guidance has become distinct from the wrong. So whoever disbelieves in Satan and believes in Allah has grasped the strong support that will never break. God is all Hearing and all Knowing. [Quran 2:256]

4. Always speak gently to your parents.

Your Lord has commanded that you should worship none but Him and show kindness to your parents. If either or both of them attain old age with you, say no word of contempt to them and do not rebuke them, but always speak gently to them. And treat them with humility and tenderness and say, "Lord, be merciful to them both, as they raised me up when I was little." [Quran Chapter 17:23-24]

5. Follow a middle path in your expenditure.

Be neither miserly nor so open-handed that you suffer reproach and become destitute. Your Lord gives abundantly to whom He wills and limited to whom He pleases. He has complete information about His servants and sees them. [Quran Chapter 17:239-30]

6. Adultery is a major sin.

And do not go near adultery, for it is an indecent thing and an evil course. [Quran 17:32]

7. There must be a group of reformers in the society.

Let there be a group among you who call others to virtue and goodness, and enjoin what is right, and forbid what is wrong: those who do this shall be successful. [Quran 3:104]

8. Pray to God. He will answer your prayer.

The Final Hour is sure to come, without a doubt, but most people do not believe it. Your Lord has said, "Call on

Me, and I will answer your prayers." But those who are too arrogant to worship Me they will undoubtedly enter the Hell in disgrace. [Quran Chapter 40: 59-60]

9. God is truly bountiful to people.

It is God who has given you the night in which to rest and the day in which to see. God is truly bountiful to people, but most people are not thankful. Such is God, your Lord, the Creator of all things. There is no god but He. How, then, are you turning away [from Him]? [Quran Chapter 40:61-62]

10. God says only, "Kun!" and it is done.

It is He who created you from clay, then from a drop of fluid, then from a tiny, clinging form, then He brought you forth as infants, then He allowed you to reach maturity, then He let you grow old, though some of you die sooner, and reach your appointed term, so that you may reflect. It is He who gives life and death, and when He ordains a thing, He says only, "Be!" and it is. [Quran Chapter 40: 67-68]

11. The Husband is the protector of his wife

Men are protectors of women because God has blessed some of them over others and because they spend their wealth on them. So virtuous women are obedient and guard in the husband's absence, which is what God would have them guard. As for those (wives) from whom you apprehend infidelity, admonish them, then refuse to share their beds, and finally give them an ultimatum. Then, if they obey you, take no further action against them. For God is High and Great. [Quran 4: 34]

12. Do not enter other's house with out permission

O' believers, do not enter other people's houses until you have asked their owners' permission and have greeted them. That will be better for you so that you may be heedful. And if you find no one at home, do not go in until permission has been granted to you. And if you are told to go back, then go back. That is more proper for you. And God knows well what you do. [Quran Chapter 24: 27-28]

13. Qualities of good Muslims

Who refrain from heinous sins and gross indecencies; and who forgive when they are angry; who obey their Lord and attend to their prayers; who conduct their affairs by mutual consultation and spend out of what We have provided for them; and when they are attacked, they defend themselves. [Quran 42: 37-39]

14. Punishment for the disbelievers

On that day, they will be dragged with iron collars and chains around their necks into the boiling water, and then they will be thrown into the Fire, and then they will be asked, "Where are those whom you associated [with God]?" They will say, "They have been lost to us, and nay, we did not invoke anything before. "Thus, God will punish the deniers of the truth. [Quran Chapter:40: 71-74]

15. God has made this earth our resting place

It is God who has given you the earth for a resting place and the heavens for a canopy. He shaped you, formed you well, and provided you with good things. Such is God, your Lord, so glory be to Him, the Lord of the Universe. He is the Living One. There is no deity save Him. So pray to Him, making religion pure for Him [only]. Praise be to God, the Lord of the Universe! [Quran Chapter 40:64-65]

16. God is the most forgiving and ever-merciful

Indeed, your Lord is the most forgiving and ever merciful towards those who do evil in ignorance and truly repent thereafter and make amends. [Quran 16:119]

17. Do not despair of God's mercy

Say, [God says] "O My servants, who have committed excesses against their souls, do not despair of God's mercy, for God surely forgives all sins. He is truly the Most Forgiving, the Most Merciful. Turn to your Lord and submit to Him before His punishment overpowers you, for then you shall not be helped. [Quran Chapter 39: 53-54]

18. Dua of true believers before their Lord

"Our Lord, do not take us to task if we forget or make a mistake! Our Lord, do not place on us a burden like the one You placed on those before us! Our Lord, do not place on us a burden we have not the strength to bear! Pardon us; and forgive us, and have mercy on us. You are our Lord and Sustainer, so help us against those who deny the truth." [Quran 2:286]

===============================

CHAPTER TEN

In the name of Allah, the most Beneficent and Merciful

1. Have faith in Allah and His Messenger.

[Say, O Muhammad]: 'O mankind! I am Allah's Messenger to you all. To Him belongs the dominion of the heavens and the earth. There is no god but He. He gives life and death. So have faith in Allah and in His Messenger, the ummi Prophet who believes in Allah and His words (the Quran), and follow him so that you may be guided to the right path.' [Quran 7:158]

2. God has created everything for the service of humanity.

It is Allah who designed for you the sea so that ships may sail upon it by His command and that you may seek His bounty so that you be grateful. And He has designed for you whatever is in the heavens and whatever is on the earth - all from Him. Indeed, there are signs of thoughtful people. [Quran Ch. 45:12-13]

3. Help orphans and needy

Have you seen one who denies the Day of Judgement? He turns away the orphan and has no urge to feed the poor. And woe to those who pray but whose hearts are not in their prayer. They do things only to show to others. And they refuse to help others. [Quran Ch 107: 1-7]

4.   All good things are made lawful for us.

If they ask you what has been made lawful for them, say, "All good things have been made lawful for you," and what you have taught your birds and beasts of prey to catch, training them as God has taught you. So eat what they catch for you, but first pronounce God's name over it. Fear God, for God is swift in taking account. [Quran 5:4]

5.   Those who disobey Allah and His Messenger shall enter the Hell.

Say, "I invoke only upon my Lord and do not associate anyone else with Him." Say, "It is not in my power to cause you either harm or good?" Say, "Surely no one can protect me against God, nor can I find besides Him any place of refuge. I only have to convey that which I receive from Him and His messages." For those who disobey God and His Messenger, there is the fire of hell, wherein they will abide forever. [Quran Chapter 72: 20-23]

6.   On Friday, rush for prayer when you hear Azan.

Believers! When the call to prayer is made on a Friday, hasten to the remembrance of God, and leave all worldly commerce: this is for your good if you but knew it. 10. And when the prayer is ended, disperse in the land and seek to obtain [something] of God's bounty; and remember God abundantly, so that you may prosper. [Quran Chapter 62]

7. Stand firmly for justice.

O' Believers! Stand firmly for justice and as witnesses to Allah, even if it goes against yourselves, your parents, or your relatives. Whether one is rich or poor, Allah takes care of both. So do not follow your desires, lest you swerve. If you deviate or turn away (from justice), then Allah is aware of what you do. [Quran 4:135]

8. God has no son or partner to share His power.

Blessed is He who sent down the Criterion (the Quran) upon His servant so that he should warn humanity. To Him alone belongs the kingdom of the heavens and the earth, and He has no son, and He never had a partner in His kingship. And He has created everything and determined its fate. And yet, instead of Him, they have made for themselves other gods that have created nothing but are themselves created. They have no power to harm or benefit them and also no power over life, death, or resurrection. [Quran Chapter 25:1-3]

9. Creation of humans and their complete life cycle

We created man from the extract of clay. Then We made him semen in a secure repository. Then, We developed the semen into a zygote. Then, We developed the zygote into an embryo. Then, We developed the embryo into bones. Then We covered the bones with flesh. Then, We developed it into a final creature. Most blessed is Allah, the Best of Creators. Then, after that, you will die. Then, on the Day of Resurrection, you will be resurrected. [Quran Chapter 23: 12-16]

10. Relationship with non-Muslims

It may well be that God will create goodwill between you and those of them with whom you are now at enmity -- for God is all-powerful, most forgiving and merciful. He does not forbid you to deal kindly and justly with anyone who has not fought you on account of your faith or driven you out of your homes: God loves the just. God only forbids you to make friends with those who have fought against you on account of your faith and driven you out of your homes or helped others to do so. Any of you who turn towards them in friendship will genuinely be transgressors. [Quran Chapter 60:7-9]

11. Among Jews and Christians, there are some upright people

They are not all alike. Among the People of the Scripture (Jews and Christians), some people are upright and virtuous; they recite Allah's revelations during the night, and they prostrate themselves before the Lord. They believe in Allah and the Last Day, advocate righteousness, forbid others from evil, and are passionate about doing good deeds. These are the righteous ones. And whatever good they do, they will not be rejected. And Allah has complete knowledge of the righteous people. [Quran Chapter 3:113-115]

12. Evidence of God is available all around us.

In the creation of the heavens and the earth; in the alternation of night and day; in the ships that sail in the ocean bearing cargoes beneficial to man; in the water which

God sends down from the sky and with which He revives the earth after its death, and in the creation of all kinds of animals; and in the courses of the winds, and in the clouds that are pressed into service between the earth and the sky, there are indeed signs for wise people. [Quran 2:164]

13. The Sun and Moon are created to serve the humanity.

It is He who sends down water from the sky. From it, you drink, and with this water grow trees on which you pasture your cattle. And with it, He grows for you crops and the olive and the date palm and the grape and all kinds of fruits. Indeed, that is a sign for a people who reflect. He has made the night and the day and the sun and the moon subservient to you, and all the stars are subservient to His command. Indeed, there are signs for men to understand this. [Quran Chapter 16:10-12]

14. Prophet Christ never said he is God

(On the Day of Judgment) Allah will ask: O' Jesus, the son of Mary, did you say to people: "Take me and my mother for gods besides Allah?" and he will answer: "Glory to You! It was not for me to say what I had no right to. Had I said so, You would surely have known it. You know all what is within my mind, whereas I do not know what is within Yours. There is no doubt that you have full knowledge of the Unseen, which is beyond our perception. I said to them nothing except what You commanded me, that is: 'worship Allah, my Lord and your Lord.' And I was aware of them as long as I remained among them; and when You did recall me, then You were witness over them. Indeed, You are a Witness to everything. If You punish them, they are Your servants; and if You forgive them, You are the All-Mighty and All-Wise."'

{Quran Chapter 5: 116-118}

==================================

CHAPTER ELEVEN

In the name of Allah, the most Beneficent and Merciful

1. **Do not compel anyone to accept Islam.**

Had your Lord pleased, all the people on earth would have believed in Him, without exception. So, will you compel people to become believers? No soul can believe except by the will of God. He will place the filth [of doubt] upon those who do not use their intelligence. [Quran Chapter 10:99-100]

2. Your wealth and children are test for you.

Indeed, Your wealth and your children are only a test, and God's reward is great: So be mindful of God as best as you can; and listen, and obey; and spend in charity: it is for your good. And those who guard themselves against their greed will surely prosper: [Quran Chapter 64:15-16]

3. **Be a giver and avoid wastefulness**

Your Lord is best aware of what is in your hearts. If you are righteous, He will indeed forgive those who relent and revert (to serving Allah). And give to the relatives, and also to people in need and people without homes, and do not squander your wealth wastefully. Indeed, spendthrifts are the brothers of Satan, and Satan is ever ungrateful to his

Lord. [Quran Chapter 17:25-27]

4. Deep thinking over nature is also a form of prayer.

Indeed, in the creation of the heavens and the earth, and the alternation of night and day, there are signs for men of understanding. Those who remember Allah while standing, sitting or (reclining) on their backs and reflecting on the creation of the heavens and the earth, (saying): 'Our Lord! You have not created this without purpose. Glory to You! Save us, then, from the punishment of the Hell. [Quran Chapter 3: 190-191]

5. Prophets also have no knowledge of the unseen

Tell them [O Muhammad]: 'I have no power to benefit or harm myself except as Allah may please. Had I known the unseen, I should have amassed all kinds of good, and no evil would have ever touched me. I am merely a warner and the herald of glad tidings to those who have faith.' [Quran Chapter 7: 188]

6. You will be returned to God after death

So, do you think that We created you uselessly and that to Us you will not be returned? "Exalted is Allah, the Sovereign, the Truth; there is no deity except Him, the Lord of the Noble Throne. And whoever invokes besides Allah another deity for which he has no reason - then his account is only with his Lord. Indeed, the disbelievers will not succeed. And, [O Muhammad], say, "My Lord, forgive and have mercy, and You are the best of the merciful." [Quran Chapter 23:115-118]

7. When will Qayamat occur?

They ask you [Prophet] about the Last Hour (Qayamat), "When will it come?" Say, "Knowledge about it rests only with my Lord; He alone will reveal when its time will come. It will be heavy on the heavens and the earth: it will suddenly overpower you." They ask you questions as if you have full knowledge of them. Say, "Knowledge about it rests only with God. But most of the people do not have any knowledge about it." [Quran 7:187]

8. The belief in Allah and good deeds are necessary for Paradise

As for those who believe and do good work, We shall admit them to Gardens through which rivers flow, wherein they will abide forever. This is a promise from God, and whose word could be more valid than God's? It is not your desires nor the desires of the People of the Book that shall prevail. Anyone who commits evil will be awarded punishment accordingly. There, he will not find any protector or patron for himself other than God. Anyone who performs good deeds, whether it is a man or woman, provided that he is a believer, shall enter Paradise. No one shall suffer the least injustice. [Quran Chapter 4: 122-124]

9. Allah and Jesus Christ are not the same.

Indeed, they are deniers of the truth who say, "God is the Christ, the son of Mary." For the Christ himself said, "O' Children of Israel, worship God, my Lord and your Lord." And if anyone associates anything with God, God will forbid him from Paradise, and Hell will be his home.

The wrongdoers shall have no one to help. [Quran 5:72]

10. Quran rejects the theory of trinity

They are deniers of the truth who say, "God is one of three." There is only One God. If they do not desist from saying so, a painful punishment is bound to befall them as they are bent on denying the truth. Why do they not turn to God and ask for His forgiveness? God is forgiving and most merciful. [Quran Chapter 5:73-74]

11. Christians are closer to Muslims than Jews and polytheists

You will find that the bitterest in their enmity to the faithful (Muslims) are the Jews and the polytheists, and the nearest in affection to them are those who say, "We are Christians." That is because there are priests and monks among them and because they are free from pride. [Quran 5:82]

12. Don't sit with the people who make fun of the Quran

When you see people engaged in finding fault with Our revelations, withdraw from them until they turn to some other topic. Should Satan cause you to forget this, then don't sit with the wrongdoers as soon as you remember. [Quran Chapter 6: 68]

13. Advise the people by the verses of the Quran.

Leave alone those who take the religion casually and lightly, and the life of this world deceives them, but you continue to remind them with the Quran, lest one is caught for his wrong deeds (in the Hereafter). There, he will have no helper or intercessor besides God. Whatever ransom they may offer, it will not be accepted. Such are those that are damned by their actions: they will have boiling water to drink and a painful punishment for their disobedience. [Quran 6:70]

14. Do's and don'ts as prescribed by Almighty God

Say, "Come! I will tell you what your Lord has really forbidden you! Do not associate anything with Him; be good to your parents; and do not kill your children for fear of poverty. We shall provide sustenance for you as well as for them; refrain from committing indecent deeds, whether openly or in secret; and do not kill the life which God has made sacred, save by law. That is what He has enjoined upon you so that you may understand. [Quran Chapter 6:151]

15. Always stand for justice.

Believers, be steadfast in the cause of God and bear witness with justice. Do not let your enmity for others turn you away from justice. Deal justly; that is nearer to being Taqwa. And fear God. Indeed, God is aware of all that you do. God has promised those who are believers and do good deeds. For them, there is forgiveness and a great reward; But those who deny the truth and deny Our commands are destined for Hell. [Quran Chapter 5:8-10]

16. Dispute among the people is natural

If your Lord had wished, He would have made humanity into one community. And there would never be any dispute. And to this end, He has created them [all], except for those to whom your Lord has shown mercy. [Quran Chapter 11:118-119]

==============================

CHAPTER TWELVE

In the name of Allah, the most Beneficent and Merciful

1. God has made the Quran easy to understand.

The Lord of Mercy will bestow affection upon those who believe and perform righteous deeds. And indeed, We have revealed the Quran in your tongue and made it easy to understand so that you may give good tidings to the God-fearing and warn the contentious people. [Quran 19:96-97]

2. Who is Almighty God?

It is He who gave you ears, eyes and hearts, yet there are a few among you who are grateful! He it is who has multiplied you on the earth, and to Him you shall all be gathered. It is He who gives life and causes death, and He controls the alternation of night and day. So will you not understand? [Quran Chapter 23:78-80]

3. Prophet Yusuf's preachings in the prison

(Prophet Yusuf said) O, my two fellow prisoners! Are many diverse lords better, or God, the One, the Almighty? All those you worship instead of Him are mere names you and your forefathers have invented. These are merely names for which God has sent down no authority: all power belongs to God alone, and He orders you to worship none but Him. This is true faith, but most people have no knowledge of it. [Quran Chapter 12:39-40]

4. Give full measure when you weigh

Give full measure when you measure, and weigh with accurate scales. That is fair and better in the end. Do not follow what you do not know, for the ear and the eye and the heart shall all be called to account. [Quran Chapter 17:35-36]

5. Don't be arrogant

Do not walk proudly on the earth. You cannot cleave the earth, nor can you rival the mountains in height. All that is evil is detestable in the sight of your Lord. [Quran Ch. 17:37-38]

6. We will be raised again after our death

Man asks, "When I am once dead, shall I be raised to life?" Does man not remember that We created him earlier when he was nothing? By your Lord, We shall most surely gather them and the devils too and bring them close to the Hell on their knees. [Quran Ch.19:66-68]

7. A terrible scene of the Hell

On that Day (Qayamat), you shall see the guilty bound in chains, Their garments shall be of pitch, and the flames of fire shall cover their faces. God will requite each soul according to its deeds. Swift is God's valuation. This is a message for humanity. Let them take warning from it and know that He is but one God. So, the people of understanding should take heed. [Quran Chapter 14:49-52]

8. Do not envy anyone

Do not envy the worldly benefits we have given to some of them. By these things, We seek only to test them. But the provision of your Lord is better and ever-lasting. [Quran 20:131]

9. Advise your family members to regular prayers

Do advise your family for prayers, and you, too, should be regular in their observance. We demand nothing from you. It is We who provide for you. And there is the best result (in the Hereafter) for the righteous people. [Quran 20:132]

10. God created all living beings from water

Do not those who deny the truth see that the heavens and the earth were joined together and that We then split them asunder? And that We have created every living thing out of water? So, will they not believe in God? [Quran 21:30]

11. Prayers provide happiness and peace of mind

So be patient with anything they may say and glorify your Lord with His praise before the rising of the sun and before its setting; and glorify Him in the hours of the night and at the beginning and end of the day, so that you may find comfort and happiness. [Quran 20:130]

12. A day with God is of one thousand years as we count

They ask you to hasten the punishment; God will never go back on His promise. A Day with your Lord is like a thousand years in your reckoning. I have given respite to many in the community who were wrongdoers. Then I seized them, and to me, they had to return. [Quran 22:47-48]

13. God created everything on the earth for humanity

Do you not see how God has made everything on the earth subservient to you and the ships that sail on the sea by His command? He holds the sky from falling on the earth, except with His will. Indeed, God is most compassionate and most merciful to humanity. It is He who gave you life. Then He will cause you to die. Then He will give you life again. Indeed, man is very ungrateful. [Quran Chapter 22: 65-66]

14. Raise questions with people about God

(O' Prophet) Ask, "To whom do the earth and all therein belong? Tell me if you have any knowledge?" They will say, "To God." Ask (them), "So why do you not get guidance? Ask, "Who is the Lord of the seven heavens and of the Glorious Throne?" They will say, "They belong to God." Ask, "So why do you not fear Him?" Ask, "In whose hands lies sovereignty over all the things? And He protects all, while none can seek protection against Him? Tell me if you have any knowledge." They will say, "All this belongs to God." Say to them, "How are you then deluded?" [Quran Chapter 23:84-89]

15. The qualities of true believers

63. The faithful servants of the Gracious One are those who walk upon the earth with humility, and when they meet the ignorant ones, their response is, "Salam" (they don't argue). 64. And they spend the night prostrating themselves and standing before their Lord. 65. They say, "Our Lord, ward off from us the punishment of the Hell, for its punishment is dreadful. 66. Indeed, it is an evil abode and evil dwelling place."

67. And when they spend, they are neither extravagant nor niggardly, but keep a balance between the two. 68. They never invoke any other deity besides God, nor take a life which God has made sacred, except with the right to do so, nor commit adultery. Anyone who does that shall face punishment. 69. He shall be doubly punished on the Day of Resurrection, and he will abide there forever in disgrace. 70. Except for those who repent and believe and do good deeds. God will change the evil deeds of such people into good ones: He is the most Forgiving and the most Merciful [Quran Chapter 25]

16. Monotheism

And invoke no god other than the God almighty, for there is no god but Him. All things are bound to perish except Him. His is the judgement, and to Him you shall be returned. [Quran 28:88]

17. Select good friends for your company

On that Day (the Day of Judgment), the wrongdoer will bite his hands and say, "Would that I had followed the

Messenger's path! Oh, would that I had never chosen such a one as companion. Certainly he strayed me from the true guidance (Quran) after it had reached me.Infact Satan is man's great betrayer." And the Messenger will say (on that day) , " Oh Lord, my people had indeed forsaken the Quran" [Quran Chapter 25:27-30]

=============================

CHAPTER THIRTEEN

In the name of Allah, the most Beneficent and Merciful

1. The Quran is undoubtedly the book of God.

This Book has, beyond all doubt, been revealed by the Lord of the Universe. Do they say, "He has prepared it himself."? No indeed! It is the truth from your Lord to warn people, to whom no warner came before you, so that they may be rightly guided. [Quran Chapter 32:2-3]

2. The advice of Prophet Luqman to his son

My dear son! Say your prayers regularly, and enjoin good, and forbid evil, and endure patiently whatever may befall you. Indeed, this is something which requires firm resolve. [Quran 31:17]

3. Three virtues for success in the Hereafter

Those who read the Book of God and attend to their prayers and spend in charity in private and in public, out of what We have provided them, may hope for a commerce that suffers no loss. He will give them their full rewards and give them more out of His bounty. Indeed, He is forgiving and appreciative. [Quran Chapter 35:29-30]

4. Whole universe is created by God alone.

It is He (Almighty God) who has made you the rulers of the earth. One who disbelieves Him shall bear the burden of his disbelief. God's displeasure with the disbelievers will only increase when they deny the truth; it will only increase their loss. Ask them, "Have you ever considered over your associate gods whom you invoke besides Allah? Could you show me what they have created on Earth? Or have they a share in the creation of the heavens?" Or have We given them a book from which they get guidance? Indeed, the wrongdoers' promises to one another are nothing but deception. [Quran Chapter 35:39-40]

5. God created heavens without any support

He has created the skies without any support that you could see, and has placed firm mountains upon the earth, lest it sway with you, and has created all types of living creatures found thereon. And We sent down water from the skies, and thus We made every kind of excellent plant grow therein. This is God's creation. Show me then what those besides Him have created! But the deniers of truth are clearly on the wrong path. [Quran Chapter 31:10-11]

6. Which signs of your Lord will you deny?

It is God who provides livestock for you, some for riding and some for your food. And for you, there are other benefits to them, too. You can reach any destination you wish on them. They carry you by land, as ships carry you on the sea. Thus, He shows you His signs; so which of the signs of God will you deny? [Quran Chapter 40:79-81]

7. The prophet's responsibility is to convey the message of God

If they turn away, then We have not sent you [O Prophet] as their guard; your responsibility is only to convey the message. Man is such that when We let him taste Our mercy, he exults in it, but if an evil befalls him which is of his own doing, he becomes utterly ungrateful. [Quran 42:48]

8. Sons and daughters are the gift of God

God has control over the heavens and the earth; He creates whatever He wants. He grants female offspring to whoever He wants and male to whoever He wants. Or both male and female. And He leaves whoever He wants childless. Indeed, He is all-knowing and all-powerful. [Quran Chapter 42:49-50]

9. Always try for peace and justice among believers

If two groups of believers fight against each other, make peace between them, and if one of them transgresses against the other, then fight the party that transgresses until it submits to the command of Allah. Then, if it complies, make peace between them with equity and act justly. Indeed, God loves those who do justice. Surely, all believers are brothers. So make peace between your brothers, and fear God so that He may be merciful to you. [Quran Chapter 49:9-10]

10. Don't ridicule each other

Believers: do not ridicule each other. It may be that the latter are better than the former, nor should women laugh at others; it may be that the latter are better than the former. And do not defame or be sarcastic to each other or call each other by [offensive] nicknames. How bad it is to earn an evil reputation after accepting the faith! Those who do not repent are evil-doers. [Quran 49:11]

11. Spying and backbiting are grave evils

Believers, avoid too much suspicion. Indeed, some suspicions are a sin. And do not spy on one another, and do not backbite. Would any of you like to eat his dead brother's flesh? No, you would hate it. Fear God; indeed, God is ever forgiving and most merciful. [Quran 49:12]

12. Who is a true believer?

The believers are only those who have faith in God and His Messenger, and they have no doubt (about them). And they strive hard with their wealth and their actions for the cause of God. They are really truthful ones. [Quran 49:15]

13. Guide people by the verses of the Quran

We know best what those who deny the truth say. You are not there to compel them, so remind them, with this Quran, to those who fear My warning. [Quran 50:45]

14. Who has created various things around you?

Have you thought about the crops you grow? Is it you who causes them to grow, or We grow them? If we want, we could turn your harvest into chaff, and then you would start lamenting, "We are ruined, and we are deprived [altogether]. "And have you thought over the water that you drink? Is it you who cause it to rain from the clouds, or do We rain it? If We want, We could make it salty. Then, why are you not grateful to me? [Quran Chapter 56: 63-70]

15. Who are the successful people?

I swear by the time, that man is surely in a state of loss, except for those who are believers and do good deeds and exhort one another to hold fast to the Truth and who exhort one another to steadfastness. [Quran Chapter 103/ 1-3]

16. Nonbelievers want you to renounce your faith

If these nonbelievers gain power over you, they will behave towards you as enemies and stretch out their hands as well as their tongues with evil intent, and they want you to renounce your faith. Neither your relatives nor your children will be of any help to you on the Day of Resurrection. He will judge between you, and God sees all that you do. [Quran Chapter 60:2-3]

17. All good things are made lawful for Muslims.

Today, all good things have been made lawful to you. The food of the People of the Book is lawful to you, and your food is lawful to them. The chaste believing women and the chaste women of the people who were given the Book before you are lawful to you. You give them their dowers and marry them, neither committing fornication nor taking them as mistresses. The deeds of anyone who rejects the faith will come to nothing, and in the Hereafter, he will be among the losers. [Quran 5:5]

18. Allah created every thing perfect

He (Allah) is the Knower of the unseen and the visible, the Powerful, the Merciful. He gave everything that He created its perfect form. And He originated the creation of humans from clay, Then, He made his progeny from an extract of a humble fluid (semen). Then He shaped him; He breathed His Spirit into him. And He blessed you with the hearing, the sight, and the hearts. But seldom you are grateful. Quran Chapter 32:6-9]

==================================

In the name of Allah, the most Beneficent and Merciful

1.   Everything in the heavens and earth praises God

All that is in the heavens and on the earth extols the glory of God. To Him belongs the Kingdom, and to Him, all praise is due, and He has power over all things. It is He who created you, but some of you are those who deny this truth, and some who believe [in it]. And God sees everything that you do. [Quran Chapter 64: 1-2]

2. God knows all that you conceal and reveal

He created the heavens and the earth for a purpose. He formed you and gave you the best of forms, and to Him you shall all return.4. He knows whatever is in the heavens and the earth. He knows all that you conceal and all that you reveal. God is aware of what is in your heart. [Quran Chapter 64:3-4]

3.   Guidance for women about social conduct and dress

(O Prophet) Say to believing women that they should lower their gaze and remain chaste and not reveal their adornments, save what usually is apparent thereof, and they should fold their shawls over their bosoms. They can only reveal their adornments to their husbands or their fathers or their husbands' fathers, or their sons or their husbands' sons, their brothers or their brothers' sons or their sisters' sons or maidservants or those whom they rightfully own, or their male attendants who have no sexual desire or children who still have no carnal knowledge of women. Nor should they walk swinging their body to draw attention to their hidden beauty. And O believers, all of you turn to God so that you may prosper. [Quran 24:31]

4. Divine advice to the wives of the Prophet

O' wives of the Prophet, you are not like any other women. If you fear God, do not be too soft-spoken (while speaking with men). It may tempt one who has a disease in his heart, but you talk to them decently. And stay in your homes and do not flaunt your charms as in the former times of ignorance. Attend to your prayers, pay zakat and obey God and His Messenger. God seeks only to remove all impurity from you, the women of the (Prophet's) household, and to make you entirely pure. [Quran 33:32-33]

5. Ettiquetes of visiting Prophet's house.

Believers! Do not enter the houses of the Prophet unless permission is given to you for a meal, and do not wait for its cooking; but when you are invited, enter, and when you have taken the meal, then disperse, do not engage in talks; surely this troubles the Prophet, but he tolerates you, and Allah does not need to tolerate the truth. And when you ask them (wives of the Prophet) for anything, ask them from behind the curtain (Hijab); this is purer for your hearts and their hearts; and it does not behove you that you should give trouble to the Apostle of Allah, nor that you should marry his wives after him ever; indeed this is a grievous thing for Allah. [Quran 33:53]

6. Instructions to Muslim women about Hijab

59. O Prophet! Say to your wives and your daughters and the women of the believers (when they are out of home) that they wear upon themselves their over-garments; this will be more proper, that they may be recognised, and thus they will not be troubled; and Allah forgives, Merciful. [Q. Chapter 33]

7. Role of Prophet Muhammad (s)

We have sent you with the truth as a conveyer of good tidings and as a warner. And you will not be held accountable for the people of Hell. [Quran 2:119]

8. Allah grants ruling power to whomever He wants.

When they met Goliath and his warriors, they said, "Our Lord, bestow patience upon us, make us stand firm, and help us against those who deny the truth." And so, by the command of God, they defeated them. David killed Goliath, and God gave him kingship and wisdom and imparted to him the knowledge of whatever He willed. Had it not been for God's repelling some people by means of others, the earth would have been filled with anarchy. But God is bountiful to His creatures. These are the revelations of God that We recite to you truly, and Indeed, you are one of the messengers of God. [Quran Chapter 2: 250-252]

9. Wisdom is the greatest blessing of God.

God is bountiful and all-knowing. He grants wisdom to whom He wants, and whoever is granted wisdom has indeed been given great wealth. Yet none bear this in mind except those endowed with understanding. [Quran 2:268-69]

10. Muslims are the best community in the world.

You are indeed the best community that has ever been brought forth for the humanity. You enjoin what is good and forbid what is evil, and you believe in God. If the People of the Book (Jews and Christians) had also considered, it would have indeed been better for them. Some of them are true believers, but most of them are disobedient. [Quran 3:110]

11. Muhammad is the messenger of God for all humanity

O' Mankind! The Messenger has brought you the truth from your Lord, so believe for your good. And if you deny the truth, know that to God belongs all that the heavens and the earth contain. God is all-knowing and wise. [Quran 4:170]

12. The Jews and the Christians are not superior to others

The Jews and the Christians say, "We are the children of God and His beloved ones." Say, "Then why does He (God) punish you for your sins? Indeed, you are but human beings among those He has created. He forgives whom He pleases and punishes whom He wills. The kingdom of the heavens and the earth and all that is between them, belong to God, and all shall return to Him." O' People of the Book (Jews and Christians), Our Messenger has come to you to make things clear to you after an interval between the messengers, lest you say, "No bearer of glad tidings and no warner has come to us." So a bearer of glad tidings and a warner (Prophet Muhammad) has indeed come to you. And God has the power over everything. [Quran Ch. 5:18-19]

13. Who is our Lord?

If God should let any harm touch you, no one could remove it except He, and if He should let some good touch you, know that He has the power to do all that He wants. He has full power and control over His servants, and He is the most Wise, the most informed. [Quran Chapter 6: 17-18]

14. Allah is the Originator of the heavens and the earth

The Originator of the heavens and the earth. How could He have a son when He has no saheba (female companion)? He created everything and is aware of everything.This is God, your Lord. There is no God but Him, the Creator of all things, so worship Him; He is the guardian of all things. [Quran Chapter 6:101-102]

15. Devils instigate people to quarrel with believers

And do not eat anything over which God's name has not been pronounced, for that indeed is disobedience. And the devils instigate their followers to argue with you. So if you obey them, you will become of those who associate partners with God. [Quran 6:121]

16. God has infused affection and mercy between husband and wife

• 85 •

And of His signs is that He created you from dust; then, you humans dispersed [throughout the earth]. And of His signs is that He created for you from yourselves, mates so that you may find tranquillity in them; and He infused between you affection and mercy. Indeed, there are signs for the thoughtful people. [Quran Chapter 30:20-21]

============================

In the name of Allah, the most Beneficent and Merciful

1. Always be God-conscious and God-fearing.

O' Believers, if you are God conscious, He will grant you the ability to discriminate between right and wrong, and He will forgive your sins, for God is great in His bounty. [Quran 8:29]

2. Always remember God to save yourself from the devil

As for one who turns away from the remembrance of the Gracious God, We appoint for him a devil, who will become his intimate companion. Devils divert men from the [right] way while they think that they are rightly guided. [Quran Chapter 43:36-37]

3. How should we respond to a greeting?

When anyone greets you, respond with a better greeting or at least return it; God takes account of all things. [Quran 4:86]

4. Usury or money-lending business is unlawful.

Those who live on usury shall rise before God like men whom Satan has demented by his touch, for they say, "Trade is only a kind of usury." But God has made trade lawful and made usury unlawful. Therefore, he who desists because of the admonition that has come to him from his Lord may retain what he has received in the past, and it will be for God to judge him. Those who revert to it shall be the inmates of the Fire; they shall abide therein forever. [Quran Chapter 2: 275]

5. Give debtors time to repay dues

Believers have a fear of God and give up what is still due to them from usury if they are true believers. If you do not do so, then know that you are at war with God and His Messenger. But if you want to recover, then you may recover your capital. Do not wrong others, and you will not be wronged. If the debtor is in difficulty, then grant him respite till a time of ease. If you were to write it off as an act of charity, that would be better for you if only you knew. [Quran Chapter 2: 278 - 280]

6. Jews and Christians should follow their divine scriptures.

Say, "People of the Book, you have no ground to stand on until you follow the Torah and the Gospel and what is revealed to you from your Lord." And what is revealed to you from your Lord will surely increase many of them in rebellion and their denial of the truth. But do not grieve for those who deny the truth. Indeed, from the Believers, Jews, Sabaeans and Christians, whoever believes in God and the Last Day and does what is right shall have nothing to fear, nor shall they grieve. [Quran Chapter 5:68-69]

7.   The blessings of God are present all around us.

It is God who created the heavens and the earth. He sends down water from the sky with which He brings forth fruits for your sustenance; He has made ships subservient to you so that they may sail across the sea by His command; and He has made the rivers for you. 33. He has also made for you the sun and the moon, both steadfastly pursuing their courses. He has made for you the night as well as the day. He has given you all that you asked of Him, and if you try to count God's favours, you will not be able to count them. Indeed, man is very unjust and ungrateful. [Quran Chapter 14: 32-34]

8.   The glory of God is witnessed everywhere.

So there is the glory of God in the evening and the morning. And His praise and glory is there in the heavens and on the earth, and in the night and at midday. He brings forth the living from the dead and the dead from the living. He gives life to the earth after its death, and you shall be raised to life in the same way. [Quran Chapter 30: 17-19]

9.   Do not abuse and revile the gods of other religions

Follow what has been revealed to you from your Lord: there is no deity but Him, and ignore the polytheists. If God had willed, they would not have associated anything with Him. And We did not appoint you over them as their protector, nor are you their guardian. And do not revile those [beings] that they invoke instead of God, lest they, in their hostility, revile God out of ignorance. Thus, We have made their actions attractive to them. Then, to their Lord, they shall all return, and He will reveal to them all that they have done. [Quran Chapter 6: 106-108]

10. Islam promotes good relations with others.

Say, " O People of the Book, let us come to a point that is common to us that we shall worship none but God and that we shall associate no partner with Him and that none of us shall take others as lords, besides God." And if they turn away, say, "Bear witness that we have submitted to God." [Quran 3:64]

11. A glimpse of the extraordinary life of the paradise

The people of Paradise shall have known provisions, the fruits of various kinds, and they shall be honourably accommodated in the Gardens of Bliss. They will be seated on the couches, facing one another. A drink will be served to them from a flowing spring. It will be white and delicious to those who drink it. It will not cause headaches or intoxication. For them, there will be spouses with modest gazes and beautiful eyes, as if they are closely guarded pearls. They will turn to one another and ask questions. [Quran Chapter37:41-50]

12. Islam is a complete religion of God for the humanity

Today, I have completed your religion for you, and my blessing is upon you. I have chosen for you Islam as your religion. [Quran 5:3)

13. Dua of Prophet Abraham

Our Lord, in you we have placed our trust and to You we turn in repentance and to You is the final return. Our Lord, do not make us a prey for those who deny the truth, and forgive us, our Lord. For You alone are the Mighty, the Wise One. Surely, there is a good example in them (Prophets) for you; for those who place their hopes in God and the Last Day. And whoever turns away should know that God is self-sufficient and worthy of all praise. [Quran Chapter 60: 4- 6]

14. Divine guidance for international relation

Those who are momin (believers) and migrated and fight in the way of God with their possessions and persons, as well as those who have given refuge and help (Muslims of Madina or Ansar), are the friends and protectors of one another. But as for those who are momin but have not migrated, you are in no way responsible for their protection until they migrate. If they seek your help in the matter of religion, it is incumbent on you to help them, provided there is a treaty between you and them. And God is witness to what you do. [Quran 8:72]

(Note: If people of other countries seek your help in the matter of religion, it can be given, provided there is such a treaty between the two countries.)

15. Repel evil with what is better

Good and evil deeds are not equal. Repel evil with what is better; then you will see that one who was once your enemy has become your dearest friend. But no one will be granted such goodness except those who exercise patience and self-restraint, and no one is granted it save those who are indeed fortunate. [Quran Chapter 41:34-35]

Xxxxxxxxxxxxxxxxxxxxxxxxxxxx

CHAPTER SIXTEEN

In the name of Allah, the most Beneficen and Merciful

1. We should worship only the God, our Creator and Sustainer.

Say, "Have you thought about those you invoke apart from God? Please show me what they have created on the earth. Or do they have a share in the heavens? Bring me a Book revealed before this or some other vestige of knowledge if you are truthful. And who is more misguided than one who invokes, besides God, such as will not answer him until the Day of Resurrection, and who are not even aware of his prayer, And when humanity gathers together (on the Day of Judgment), they will become their enemies and deny their worship? [Quran Chapter 46: 4-6]

2. No one can write a book like the Quran.

Say, "If all men and jinn gathered together to produce the like of this Quran, they could not produce one like it, even if they helped one another." In this Quran, We have narrated all kinds of examples for the people, yet most of them persist in denying the truth. [Quran Chapter 17: 88-89]

3. On Judgment day, no father will help his son

O' humanity, seek protection with your Lord and fear the Day when neither will the father be of any avail to his son nor will the son be of any avail to his father. God's promise is undoubtedly true. So let not worldly life beguile you, nor let the Deceiver (Satan) deceive you concerning God. [Quran 31:33]

4. Don't be arrogant and boastful.

O' my dear son! Say your prayers regularly, and enjoin good, and forbid evil, and endure patiently whatever may befall you. Indeed, this is something which requires firm resolve. Do not avert your face from people out of haughtiness, and do not walk with pride on the earth: for, behold, God does not love arrogant and boastful people. And walk modestly and lower your voice, for the ugliest of all voices is the braying of the ass." [Quran Chapter 31:17-19]

5. The Quran is guidance and cure for internal vices

O' Mankind! There has come to you an admonition from your Lord, a cure for what is in the hearts, and a guide and a blessing to the true believers. [Quran 10:57]

6. Regular prayers restrain us from evils.

Recite what has been revealed to you in the book, and pray regularly. Indeed, prayer restrains one from indecency and evil, and remembrance of God is the greatest. God knows all your actions. [Quran 29:45]

7. Be obedient to God, His Messenger and the authorities

O' Believers obey God and obey the Messenger and those who have been entrusted with authority among you.

If you are in dispute over any matter, refer it to God and the Messenger. If you genuinely believe in God and the Last Day, this is best and best in the end. [Quran 4:59]

8.   Do not ascribe partners to Allah

God will not forgive anyone for associating something with Him, while He will forgive whoever He wishes for anything besides that. Whoever ascribes partners to God is guilty of a great sin. [Quran 4:48]

9.   God has permitted all Good things to be eaten

Say, "Who has forbidden the adornment of God, which He has brought forth for His servants and good things, clean and pure, which God has provided for His servants?" Say, "They are [lawful] for the believers in the present life, and they shall be exclusively for them on the Day of Resurrection." Thus, We explain Our signs to the people who understand. Say, "My Lord has forbidden indecency, both open and hidden, sin and wrongful oppression without due reason, and He has also forbidden that you associate things with Allah for which He has provided no reason and that you say things about Him without knowledge.
[Quran Chapter 7:32-33]

10.   All intoxicating items and gambling are prohibited.

They ask you [Prophet] about intoxicants and gambling. Say, "There is great sin in both, although they have some benefit for people, but their harm is greater than their benefit." They ask you what they should spend [in God's cause]. Say, "Whatever is surplus to your needs." Thus, God makes His commandments clear to you so that you may reflect [Quran 2:219]

11. List of some prohibited items for Muslims

He has forbidden you only carrion, blood and the flesh of swine; also anything consecrated in the name of any but God. But if anyone is forced by dire necessity, not desiring it or exceeding his immediate need, God is forgiving and merciful towards him. And do not falsely declare, "This is lawful, and this is forbidden," so as to fabricate a lie against God. Indeed, those who fabricate a lie against God shall not prosper. [Quran Chapter 16:115-116]

12. God enjoins Believers to spend on charity.

O' Believers, spend out of what We have given you before the Day comes when there will be neither trading, friendship, nor intercession. Honestly, those who deny the truth are the wrongdoers. [Quran 2:254]

13. Be good to your parents, relatives and others.

Worship God and do not associate partners with Him. And be good to your parents, to relatives, to orphans, to people in need, and the neighbour who is a relative, and the neighbour who is not related to you and your companions and the wayfarers and those who are your subservient. God does not like arrogant, boastful people. [Quran 4:36]

14. Don't spoil your charity with hurtful words.

O' Believers, do not spoil your charitable deeds with reminders and hurtful words, like one who spends his wealth to show people and who does not believe in God and the Last Day. They are like a rock covered with earth: a shower falls upon it and leaves it stiff and bare. They will gain nothing from their work. God does not guide those who deny the truth. [Quran 2:264]

15. Fight with those who fight against you

And fight in God's cause against those who wage war against you, but do not commit aggression, for indeed, God does not love aggressors. Fight them wherever you find them [those who fight against you]; drive them out of the places from which they drove you, for [religious] persecution is worse than killing. Do not fight them at the Sacred Mosque unless they fight you there. If they do fight you, fight them. Such is the reward for those who deny the truth. [Quran Chapter 2: 190-191]

16. God does not like misers and spendthrifts.

Those who are miserly and enjoin others to be the same and conceal the riches which God has given them of His bounty, We have prepared a humiliating punishment for such disbelievers. And [God does not like] those who spend their wealth for the sake of ostentation, who do not believe in God or the Last Day. And whoever has Satan as his companion has an evil companion. [Quran Chapter 4: 37-38]

17. Avoid intoxicants and gambling.

O'believers, intoxicants gambling and [consecrated] stones and divining arrows are abominations devised by

Satan. Avoid them so that you may prosper. Satan seeks to sow enmity and hatred among you by means of wine and gambling and to keep you away from the remembrance of God and from your prayers. Will you not then abstain? [Quran Chapter 5:90-91]

18. Call towards the path of your Lord with wisdom

Call to the way of your Lord with wisdom and fair exhortation and reason with them in the best way. Your Lord knows best those who have strayed away from His path, and He knows best those who are rightly guided. [Quran 16:125]

19. Attributes of Almighty God

God: there is no deity save Him, the Living, the Eternal One. Neither slumber nor sleep overtakes Him. To Him belong whatsoever is in the heavens and whatsoever is on the earth. Who can intercede with Him except by His permission? He knows all that is before them, and all that is behind them. They can grasp only that part of His knowledge which He wills. His throne extends over the heavens and the earth, and their upholding does not weary Him. He is the Sublime, the Almighty One! [Quran 2:255]

=========================

CHAPTER SEVENTEEN

Prophet Muhammad (s) and the Holy Quran

While reading the Quran, we find many verses that deal with the life, the mission and the character of Prophet Mohammad (saw). Here, we would like to mention a few.

1. **Prophet Muhammad a role model for Muslims**

Indeed, for you and those who believe in God and the Last Day and who always remember God, there is a good example in the life of the Prophet of Allah. (Quran 33:21)

2. Role of the Prophet as a messenger of God

It is He who has raised among the Ummi (inhabitants of Makkah) a messenger from among themselves, who recites His revelations to them, and purifies them, and teaches them the Book and wisdom, for they had been clearly misguided earlier. (Quran 62:2)

(Note: Ummi also means unlettered and those who were not blessed with the Holy Scriptures.)

3. **The Prophet (s) is mentioned in the Torah and the Gospel**

Those who follow the messenger - the unlettered Prophet, find him mentioned in the Torah and the Gospel that are with them. He commands them to do right and forbids them to do wrong. He makes good things lawful to them and bad things unlawful. And he relieves them of their burdens and yokes that are upon them. So those who believe in him, honour him, help him, follow the light (Quran) which is sent down with him, it is they who will prosper." (Quran 7:157)

4. Prophet (s) was gentle with the people

It is by God's grace that you are gentle with them, for if you were harsh and hard-hearted, they would indeed have deserted you. So bear with them, pray for their forgiveness, and consult them regarding the conduct of affairs. And when you have made a decision, trust in God. Indeed, God loves those who trust him. (Quran 3:159)

5. Prophet (s) was deeply concerned about people's welfare

There has come to you a messenger from amongst yourselves. It grieves him that you should perish. He is deeply worried about your welfare and is full of kindness and mercy towards believers. (Quran 9:128)

6. Prophet (s) was a human being

Say, I am only a human being like you. It is revealed to me that your God is one God. So let him who hopes to meet his Lord do good deeds, and let him associate no one else in the worship of his Lord. (Quran 18:110)

7.   Prophet (s) did not know the Ghaib (Unseen)

(O' Prophet: Say, I do not say to you that I possess the treasures of God, nor do I know the unseen (Ghaib) nor do I tell you that I am an angel. I follow only that which is revealed to me. Ask, are the blind and the seeing alike? So why can you not think? (Quran 6:50)

8.   Prophet (s) was sent for the whole of humanity.

We have sent you as a bearer of glad tidings and a Warner for the whole of humanity, but most people do not know. (Quran 34:28)

==========================

CHAPTER EIGHTEEN

<u>The Final Sermon of Prophet Mohammad (pbuh)</u>
(From the summit of Arafat on the occasion of Hajjtul wida)
After praising and thanking God, the Prophet (pbuh), said

- "O People, lend me an attentive ear, for I know not whether, after this year, I shall ever be amongst you again. Therefore, listen to what I am saying to you very carefully and take these words to those who could not be present here today.
- O People, just as you regard this month, this day, this city as Sacred, so consider the life and property of every Muslim as a sacred trust.
- Please return the goods entrusted to you to their rightful owners.
- Hurt no one so that no one may hurt you.
- Remember that you will indeed meet your Lord and that He will indeed judge your deeds.
- God has forbidden you to take usury. Therefore, all usury obligations shall henceforth be waived. Your capital, however, is yours to keep. You will neither inflict nor suffer any inequity.
- God has decreed that there shall be no usury and that all the usury due to Al-Abbas ibn Abd'el Muttalib shall

henceforth be waived...

- Beware of Satan for the safety of your religion. He has lost all hope that he will ever be able to lead you astray in big things, so beware of following him in small things.
- O People, you indeed have certain rights with regard to your wives, but they also have rights over you. Remember that you have taken them as your wives only under the trust of God and with His permission. If they abide by your right, then to them belongs the right to be fed and clothed in kindness.
- Treat your wives well and be kind to them, for they are your partners and committed helpers.
- And it is your right that they do not make friends with any one of whom you disapprove, as well as never to be unchaste.
- O People, listen to me in earnest, worship only God, perform your five daily prayers, fast during the month of Ramadan, and offer Zakat. And perform Hajj if you have the means.
- All humanity is born from Adam and Eve.
- An Arab has no superiority over a non-Arab, nor does a non-Arab have any superiority over an Arab; a white has no superiority over a black, nor does a black have any superiority over a white; [none have superiority over another] except by piety and good action.
- Learn that every Muslim is a brother to every Muslim and that the Muslims constitute one brotherhood. ?Nothing shall be legitimate to a Muslim which belongs to a fellow Muslim unless it was given freely and willingly. Do not, therefore, do injustice to yourselves.
- Remem011ber, one day, you will appear before God and answer for your deeds. So beware, do not stray from the path of righteousness after I am gone.

- O People, no prophet or apostle will come after me, and no new faith will be born. Reason well, therefore, O people, and understand the words which I convey to you.
- I leave behind two things, the Quran and my example, the Sunnah, and if you follow these, you will never go astray.
- All those who listen to me shall pass on my words to others and those to others again, and it may be that the last ones understand my words better than those who listen to me directly.
- Be my witness, O God, that I have conveyed your message to your people."

Thus, the beloved Prophet completed his Final Sermon, and upon it, near the summit of Arafat, the revelation came down:

"...This day have I perfected your religion for you, completed My Grace upon you, and have chosen Islam for you as your religion..." (Quran 5:3)

Though the Prophet's soul has left this world, his words are still living in our hearts.

Xxxxxxxxxxxxxxxxx